Happy
St. Patrick's
Day !

T is for: Top Hat!

P is for: Pot of Gold !

Help the silly sheep

find the lucky clover!

C is for: Celtic crosses !

Kiss Me
I'm Irish !

Count the number of leaves on each clover

Help the leprechaun

find his top hat!

L

is for:
Leprechaun!

I is for: Ireland!

Northern Ireland

Irish Sea

Ireland

North Atlantic Ocean

DUBLIN

St. George's Channel

Happy St. Patrick's Day!

Can you circle 5 differences between the Leprechauns?

S is for: Shamrocks!

F

is for:

Flag of Ireland !

↑ **Green**   ↑ **White**   ↑ **Orange**

H is for: Horseshoes!

Good Luck

S is for: Silly Sheep!

Help the rainbow

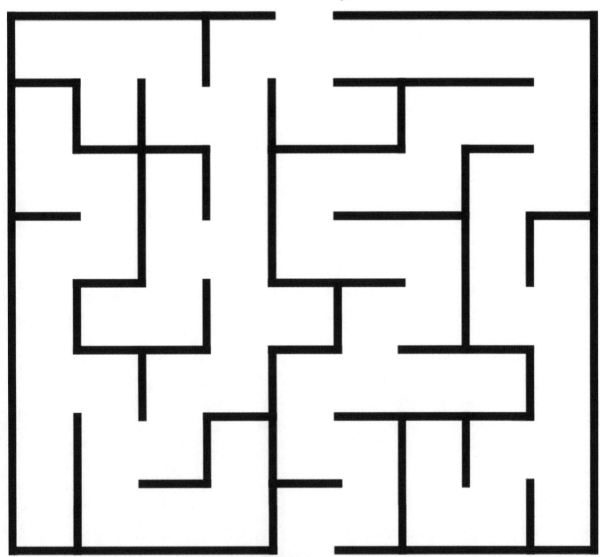

 find the pot of gold!

K is for: Knot!

G is for: Green Ribbon!

Happy 🍀 🍀
St. Patrick's Day!

Made in the USA
San Bernardino, CA
04 March 2020